On the Move

~ *Joy Richardson* ~

FRANKLIN WATTS

NEW YORK • LONDON • SYDNEY

© 1998 Franklin Watts

Franklin Watts
96 Leonard Street
London EC2A 4RH

Franklin Watts Australia
14 Mars Road
Lane Cove
NSW 2066

ISBN: 0 7496 3018 3

10 9 8 7 6 5 4 3 2 1

Dewey Decimal Classification Number: 758

A CIP catalogue record for this book is
available from the British Library.

Editor: Sarah Ridley
Design: White Design
Art Director: Robert Walster

Photographs:
© The Ashmolean Museum, Oxford pgs 4-5, 26 (top); © by Courtesy of the Trustees of
the British Museum pgs 16-17; © The Courtauld Institute front cover, pgs 22-23;
© Kunsthistorisches Museum, Vienna pgs 8-9, 27; reproduced by courtesy of the Trustees
of the National Gallery, London pgs 10-11, 18-19, 20-21, 28, 30, 31;
© Prado Museum pgs 14-15; Rochdale City Art Gallery/Bridgeman Art Library -
'Our Town' reproduced by courtesy of Mrs Carol Ann Danes pgs 24-25;
V&A Picture Library pgs 6-7, 26(bottom); reproduced by permission of the
Trustees of the Wallace Collection pgs 12-13.

Printed in Belgium

Contents

*How do bodies change shape as they
walk, run, bend and stretch?
How do you show wind, rain and water
on the move?*

Explore the pictures in this book to discover some artists'
ways of showing stillness and movement.

The Hunt in the Forest
painted by Uccello (detail)

People, horses and dogs
jump and run, chasing deer
into the deep, dark forest.

Dogs leap forward
with bodies stretched.

Legs bend and arms swing to help people run.

Who is going forward and who is stopping?

Night Attack on a Town
painted by Zamar

Enemy soldiers ride up to the town.
People fight to keep them out.

Horses prance in
front of the gate.

Archers twang
their bows.

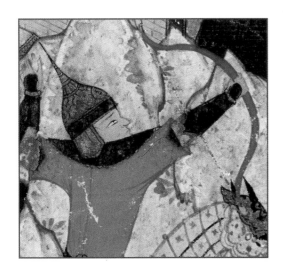

Raised
arms hurl
down rocks.

Will this shield
protect him?

Children's Games

painted by Bruegel

Two hundred children are on the go.
Legs, arms, heads and bodies
all join in the play.

Look for children ...

upside
down ...

twirling
round ...

and
playing
leap-frog.

Who's about to fall off?

A Winter Scene with Skaters
painted by Avercamp

Everyone is out skating and enjoying themselves.

Look out for people ...

kneeling down ...

toppling over ...

sliding along ...

and dancing on the ice.

The Swing
painted by Fragonard

A fine young lady swings
to and fro under the trees.

Her pink dress
billows in the air.

She holds
on to the
rope.

He's holding
on too.

She stretches her leg ...
and kicks off her shoe.

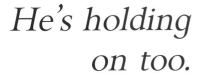

Will her friend catch it?

Boys Climbing a Tree
painted by Goya

Three boys are helping each
other to climb a tree.

Hands press down
to bear the weight.

You can see
the back of
a grimy
foot.

One leg
grips the
trunk.

A friend holds on and watches.

The Hollow of the Deep Sea Wave

colour print by Hokusai

Surging, foaming
waves curl and crash
as boats cut through the water.

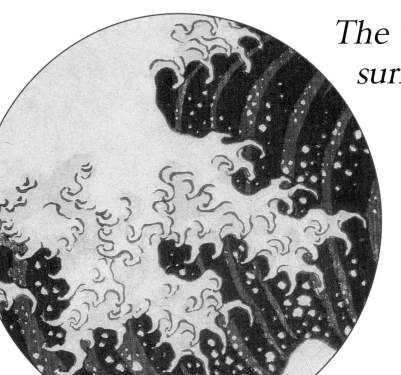

The wave rears up with
surf like dragon claws.

The waves frame
a snow-capped
mountain.

How many people can
you see in boats?

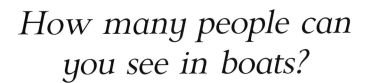

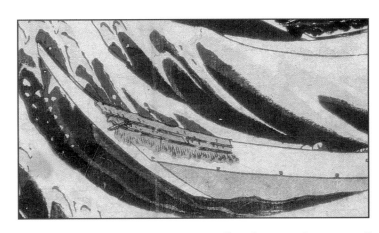

Where is the end of this boat?

La La at the Cirque Fernando
painted by Degas

Degas loved painting people in action,
such as this acrobat high in the circus dome.

Can you see her hanging
on by her teeth?

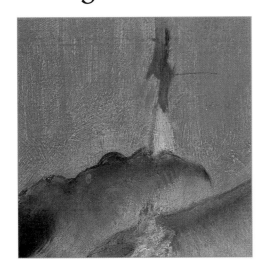

She balances with her
arms flung out.

Look how she
bends her knees ...

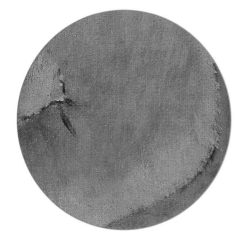

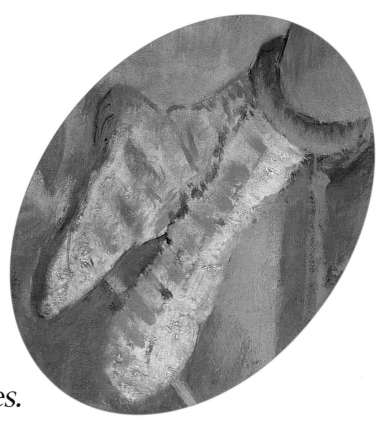

crosses her ankles
and points her toes.

Tropical Storm with a Tiger
painted by Rousseau

The tiger is on the move through the forest as the rain lashes down.

Can you see rain and lightning?

Follow the leaves to see which way the wind is blowing.

The tiger bounds through the undergrowth.

Look at its legs.

Study for Le Chahut

painted by Seurat

The dancers whirl as the music plays.
Seurat turns it all into dots of colour.

Her head leans back
as she kicks up high.

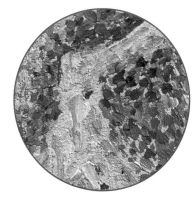

Look at the
hands holding
swirling skirts.

Can you match the
legs on the ground ...

to the legs in the air?

Our Town
painted by Lowry

People hurry busily along or
stand and watch
as the world goes by.

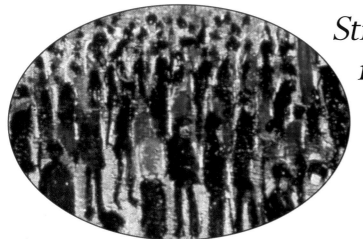

Strokes and dabs of brown make a bustling crowd.

People walk briskly, leaning forwards.

Arms and legs stand out against the white background.

Little dogs look on.

Moving Parts

Knees bend

Look how legs bend when people run.

Try painting a group of runners to show what happens.

For help, look back at page 4.

Arms stretch

How do arms move when running, throwing, reaching out or holding on?

Try painting one of these actions with the arms in the right place.

For help, look back at pages 6 and 14.

Bending bodies

Bodies lean forwards or backwards, or twist or bend when people are on the move.

Paint a playground full of people, showing the shapes their bodies make as they play.

For help, look back at pages 8, 10 and 14.

Two legs or four

How do animals move their legs?

Try painting a cat, a horse or a dog on the move.

For help, look back at pages 4 and 20.

Seeing a pattern

Bodies on the move make interesting shapes.

Make a simple drawing of someone running, dancing or playing a game.

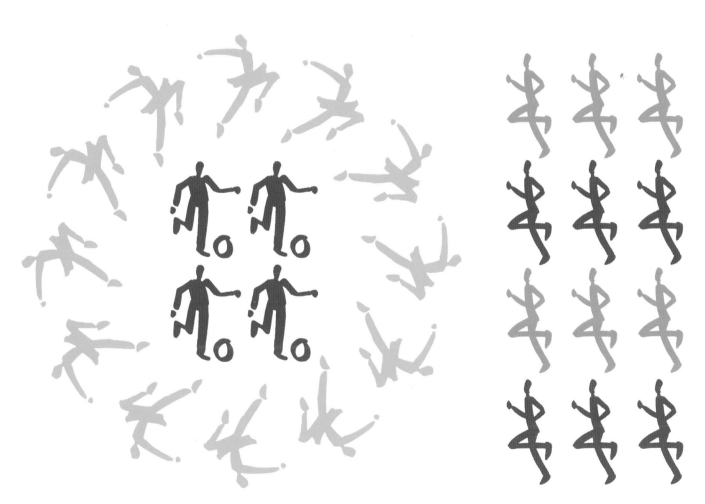

Repeat it to make an interesting pattern.
For help, look back at pages 22 and 24.

More about the pictures in this book

■ The Hunt in the Forest

Paolo Uccello (1397-1475) lived in Florence. In this picture he patterns the darkness with bright, moving figures. He was fascinated by the use of perspective and arranged the whole scene to draw your eye into the forest in pursuit of the deer.

■ Children's Games

Pieter Bruegel (about 1525-1569) lived in Holland. He had two sons, Jan and Pieter the Younger, who also became famous painters. He enjoyed painting the ordinary activities of village life and he looked back with humour to the fun and games of his own childhood.

■ Night Attack on a Town

This picture is an illustration from 'The Book of Victory' by Nafar Zamar which celebrates the conquests of a Mogul Emperor. The Mogul Empire expanded in the sixteenth and seventeenth centuries to control much of India.

■ A Winter Scene with Skaters Near a Castle (full title)

Hendrick Avercamp (1585-1634) lived in Holland, where low, flat land often flooded and froze in winter. Avercamp liked painting everyone coming out to enjoy themselves on the ice. He could not speak himself and perhaps this made him observe life more sharply.

■ The Swing

Jean Honore Fragonard (1732-1806) was a popular painter in Paris before the French Revolution. People liked his playful pictures of leisure and luxury. Here a rich and fashionable young lady is teasing a suitor by kicking off her shoe for him to catch.

■ Boys Climbing a Tree

Francisco de Goya (1746-1828) was Spanish. Goya often painted children, dressed up in their best for smart portraits, or simply playing naturally. This picture was one of a series painted on cardboard as designs for tapestries to be made at the royal factory.

■ The Hollow of the Deep Sea Wave

Katsushika Hokusai (1760-1849) was a Japanese artist. He responded to nature with simple but striking designs and colours. This colour print is one of his 'Thirty-six views of Mount Fuji'. It shows the old volcano, the highest peak in Japan, seen through the hollow of a huge wave.

■ La La at the Cirque Fernando

Edgar Degas (1834-1917) lived in Paris and loved painting entertainers at work. This picture shows an unusual view of La La, a circus acrobat who was famous for her strength, hanging from a wire by her teeth.

■ Tropical Storm with a Tiger

Henri Rousseau (1844-1910) learned all he could about exotic plants and animals without ever leaving France. He created this fantasy forest from his imagination, making a rich pattern of shapes and colours. He borrowed the tiger from a picture by another artist.

■ Study for Le Chahut

Georges Seurat (1859-1891) was a French painter. He was interested in how our eyes see colour and experimented with using separate dots or strokes of colour to create an overall impression. He made this picture of high-kicking cabaret dancers as preparation for another painting.

■ Our Town

L S Lowry (1887-1976) lived in the north of England. He found beauty in city streets and crowds, factory buildings and smoking chimneys. He looked on as nameless people scurried about their business and painted them as dark figures against a light background.

Index